THE HISTORY DETECTIVE
INVESTIGATES LOCAL HISTORY

Martin Parsons

WAYLAND

Editor: Jason Hook
Designer: Simon Borrough

First published in 1997 by Wayland Publishers Ltd, 61 Western Road, Hove, East Sussex, BN3 1JD, England.

© Copyright 1997 Wayland Publishers Ltd

British Library Cataloguing in Publication Data
Parsons, Martin
    The history detective: investigates local history
    1. Local history - Research - Juvenile literature 2. History
    – Sources – Juvenile literature
    I. Title
    907.2

ISBN 0 7502 2043 0

Printed and bound in Italy by G. Canale & CSpA, Turin.

Cover picture: Little Moreton Hall, Congleton, Cheshire.

Picture Acknowledgements: The publishers would like to thank the following for permission to reproduce their pictures: David Beasley, Pie Powder Press 24(bottom), 25(bottom); Peter Cox, Fotosparks 7(bottom-left), 17, 24(top), 25(top), 40(bottom); James Davis Travel 36; Edinburgh Central Library 12, 13, 15; Eye Ubiquitous 41(top); Robert Harding *cover*, 4, 32; Huntly House, Edinburgh 9; Oxford Picture Library 8; Edward Parker 5; Martin Parsons 26, 27; Popperfoto 22; Sheffield City Museums 19(bottom); Tony Stone 33, 44; Topham 7(bottom-right), 20, 21, 41(bottom), 43, 45; Wayland Picture Library 1, 6, 7(top), 19(top), 23, 37, 38, 39, 40(top), 42; Welsh Industrial and Maritime Museum 28, 29, 30, 31.
Cartoon bloodhound by Richard Hook.
Illustrations on pages 34, 35 and 37 by John Yates.

'To my nephew Ross Parsons and my god-daughter Annabel Borthwick. May they grow up to enjoy the fun and excitement of history.' Martin Parsons.

CONTENTS

INTRODUCTION

Have you ever wanted to be Sherlock Holmes? If he and other detectives, both real and in books, want to find out who committed a crime they need to search for as many clues as possible. In the same way, historians are a kind of detective. We have to look for signs to show us what might have happened at a certain time in the past.

At school, you may find a lot of history information in books, but you cannot always do this with local history. Instead, *you* have to be the detective, and search for the clues and evidence available in your area.

This book will show you how to become a history detective investigating your own local history. It will help you to uncover the hidden clues to our past which lie all around us. These clues will be very important if you are asked to do a history project for school. They will help you to build up a picture of what life was like in the past.

Many people in Kent live in 'oast houses' like this one. For a history detective, these strange buildings hold clues to an industry which was important to Kent's past.

HOP FIELDS

To help you with your own project, our cartoon detective, the bloodhound Sherlock Bones, will show you how to:
– choose a history mystery to investigate
– develop your history detective skills
– find the missing clues
– take shortcuts and save time
– take notes and write up your project

Bones will show you that picking up and following your own scent of the past, rather than using other people's work, can be very enjoyable. By the end of the book, you should be able to gather all your evidence and write it up into a detailed report – just like a real detective.

Wherever you see a paw-print like this, you will find a mystery to solve – to help you practise your detective skills. The answers can all be found on page 47.

🐾 What are the objects on the shield, on the pub sign shown below?

🐾 What historic industry in Kent do you think the oast house, the signpost and the pub sign tell us about? (There are more clues on page 44)

ISLE OF DOGS

This pub sign in Kent also holds clues to the county's industrial history.

CHOOSING YOUR TOPIC

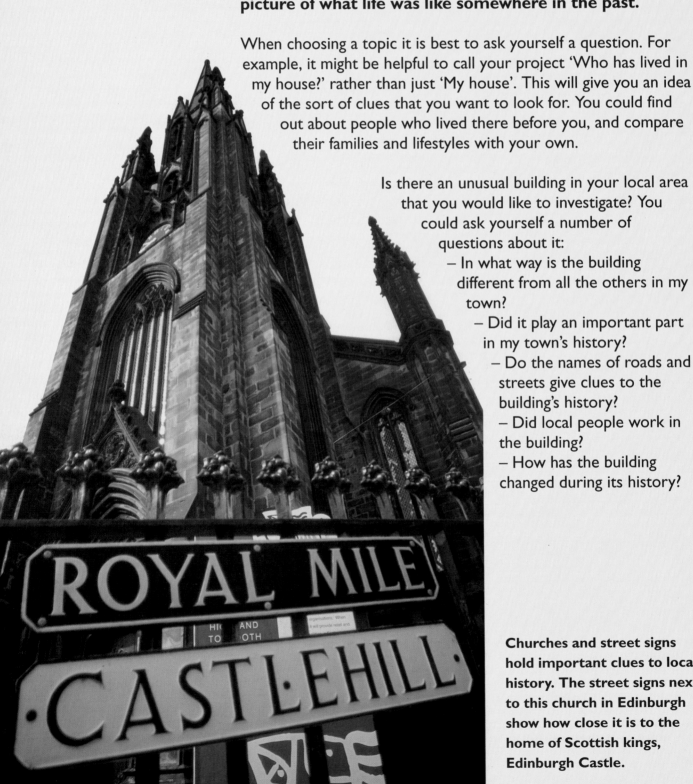

You will find your project more enjoyable if you choose a small, local topic to investigate. This way you can gather enough clues to form a detailed picture of what life was like somewhere in the past.

When choosing a topic it is best to ask yourself a question. For example, it might be helpful to call your project 'Who has lived in my house?' rather than just 'My house'. This will give you an idea of the sort of clues that you want to look for. You could find out about people who lived there before you, and compare their families and lifestyles with your own.

Is there an unusual building in your local area that you would like to investigate? You could ask yourself a number of questions about it:
– In what way is the building different from all the others in my town?
– Did it play an important part in my town's history?
– Do the names of roads and streets give clues to the building's history?
– Did local people work in the building?
– How has the building changed during its history?

Churches and street signs hold important clues to local history. The street signs next to this church in Edinburgh show how close it is to the home of Scottish kings, Edinburgh Castle.

Old newspapers are full of history clues.

Notice how other questions lead on from your original one, like a trail of clues. These questions can provide a framework for your topic because you can simply set out to answer each one in turn.

Other starting points for your investigation could be:
– Does my town's name give a clue to its history?
– Why does a road have a certain name?
– Who does a local statue represent?
– How did a public house get its name?

Choose a topic or mystery that you can study by looking at 'primary sources' – things from the past like buildings, monuments, old newspapers, photographs – rather than by using 'secondary sources' like modern books. Your project should be fun for you to investigate and interesting for those who will read your report. Above all, choose a topic that you think you will enjoy!

🐾 **What type of building do you think once existed near the street signs shown below? The newspaper and pub sign are extra clues.**

These street signs can all be found in the town of Reading.

This pub sign might give you a clue to the building that once existed nearby.

COLLECTING CLUES

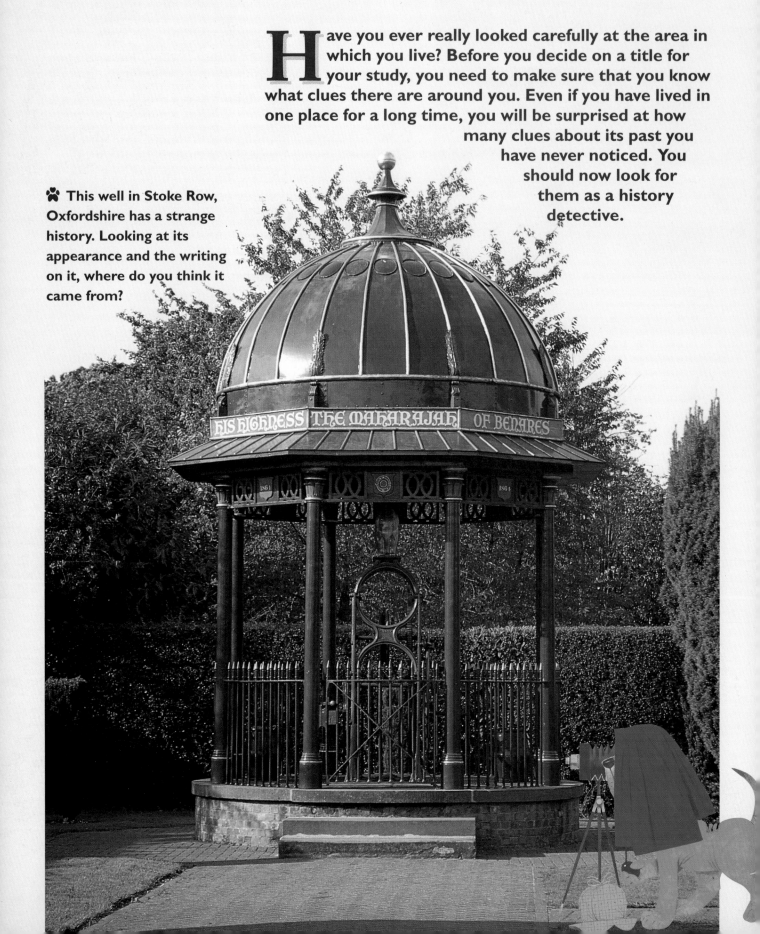

Have you ever really looked carefully at the area in which you live? Before you decide on a title for your study, you need to make sure that you know what clues there are around you. Even if you have lived in one place for a long time, you will be surprised at how many clues about its past you have never noticed. You should now look for them as a history detective.

🐾 This well in Stoke Row, Oxfordshire has a strange history. Looking at its appearance and the writing on it, where do you think it came from?

HIS HIGHNESS THE MAHARAJAH OF BENARES

1861   1864

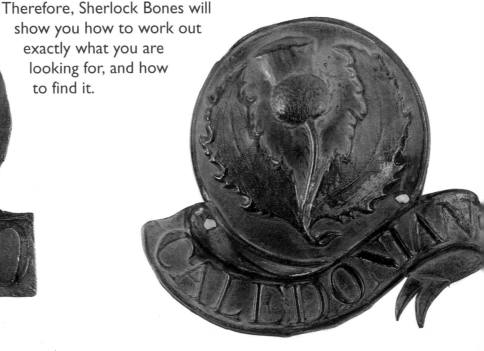

An easy way of finding clues is to go for a walk and keep your eyes open for anything that looks historical or unusual. It may be useful for your project. If possible, take a camera with you and a sketch pad for making quick, simple drawings and writing down information. If you have a small tape recorder, you could carry it with you and record details about interesting buildings. Remember, a historian needs to be like a detective and search carefully for important evidence.

Information gained from what you see may be a good starting point for your project. Some information, though, cannot be discovered this easily. In order to find out more details, you need to look up facts and evidence in old books, documents and other sources. But where do you find them?

Most old documents from industries, parish councils and schools are stored in libraries and Record Offices. It would be an impossible task to look at all the records of your area. It would take too much time and you might not find anything at all. Therefore, Sherlock Bones will show you how to work out exactly what you are looking for, and how to find it.

🐾 Signs like these, from Huntly House in Edinburgh, were seen on many houses after the seventeenth century. Looking at the blazing sun and the words 'British Fire Office', what do you think they were used for?

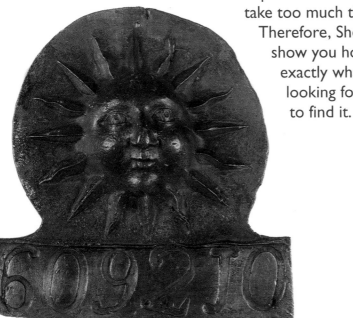

SEARCHING THE RECORD OFFICE

We will imagine that you want to look at a logbook from your local primary school (we will look at logbooks in detail on page 20). Logbooks are usually kept in your local Record Office. You can find the Record Office in the main town in your area, where the county or regional council has its offices. To find the logbook, you should follow the same steps as Sherlock Bones:

1. Look up the name of your county council in the telephone directory. There will be a lot of telephone numbers listed there, and you need to find the one marked 'Record Office'. Now you can telephone the office to make an appointment and reserve a desk. When you phone, you can ask the 'archivist' who looks after the documents whether or not they have the logbook that you want. This may save you a wasted journey.

2. Go to the Record Office at the time arranged. When you arrive, the archivist will show you to your desk. You will be given a reader's ticket which you need to sign. You can keep this ticket and use it on future visits.

3. Some offices have their documents listed on computer. If they do not, you will need to look at two sets of index cards.

If you were looking for the 1880 logbook for Crookham School in the parish of Thatcham in Berkshire, you would find the following index cards:

Parish Index

THATCHAM — **School Records**

1864-1964	Logbooks of Thatcham Church of England School	C/EL 53/1, 2-6
1875-1957	Logbook of Crookham School	C/EL 36/1-3
1794-1860	Minutes and Accounts of Lady Winchcombe's Charity School	D/P 130/25/6
1913-1955	School Manager's minutes	C/EM 19, 67
1900-1957	Crookham C of E (Controlled) School	C/EZ 7
1945-1946	Registers of British School, Senior, Junior and Infant departments	C/ER 32

The Parish Index lists the county's parishes in alphabetical order. If you know which parish your school is in, you can find it in this index.

The Subject Index contains a list of subjects in alphabetical order. The school logbook can be found under the heading 'Education'.

Subject Index

C/EL/Education:School Logbooks 3-Berkshire Record Office.

29	Burghfield Common (Mrs Bland's)	1 vol.	1873-1905
30/1,2	Didcot, The Manor School, C of E	2 vols.	1881-1903
31	Didcot, Board (Evening School)	1 vol.	1896-1904
32	Didcot, Board (Infant's Class)	1 vol.	1887-1918
33	Woolhampton, C of E		
34/1,2	Maidenhead, Boyne Hill	2 vols.	1866-1905
35/1,2	East Hagbourne, C of E	2 vols.	1875-1954
36/1-3	Crookham (parish of Thatcham)	3 vols.	1875-1957

🐾 What is the reference number for the logbook that we want? It can be found in both indexes.

Having found the reference number, you need to fill in a request form and hand it in at the desk. The archivist will find the logbook and bring it to you. You can then search it for clues.

Some documents, such as censuses and street directories, are found in your local library and not the Record Office. Tracking them down will be another important part of your detective work.

STREET DIRECTORIES

If you live in an old house, who lived there before you? If you live on a new estate, what was there before the houses were built? You can investigate both of these questions by looking at another sort of document, called a street directory.

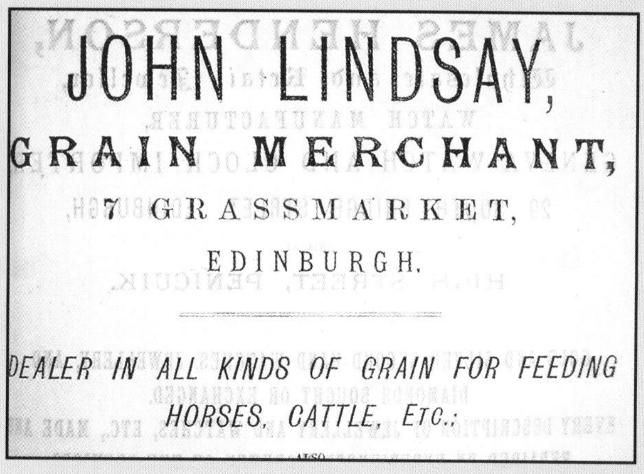

You can find street directories in your local reference library. They were published every year from the early 1800's until today. They contain advertisements for shops and local industries, which will give you an idea of the goods and services on offer in the past.

Most importantly, the directories provide history detectives with a list of houses in each street, the name of each householder and sometimes their trade. This gives you another clue about the major industries and crafts in an area.

JOHN LINDSAY,

GRAIN MERCHANT,

7 GRASSMARKET,

EDINBURGH.

DEALER IN ALL KINDS OF GRAIN FOR FEEDING HORSES, CATTLE, ETC.;

This advert (above) from the Edinburgh and Leith street directory of 1883 shows that John Lindsay ran a business at number 7, Grassmarket, selling feed for horses.

Look at the following examples, taken from the 'Edinburgh and Leith' street directories of 1882-3 and 1883-4. The Grassmarket is an area in the heart of old Edinburgh:

Grassmarket, Edinburgh 1882-3

1	Richardson, Francis, & Co		60	M'Donald, Angus, saddler
5	Scott, James, & Co		58	Rose, William, saddler
7	Lindsay, John		56	Edinburgh Rope, Bag, and Twine Store
9	Spence, Joseph, saddler		54	Wilkinson, John
11 & 13	Spence, Henry B.		54	Thomson's Court
15	Traynor, John, rag merchant		54	M'Ewan, Robert
19	McCallum, Alexander Inglis		52	Forgan, David, grocer
23	Moyes, James		50	Weir, John
25	Croan, James		48	Binnie, A., spirit dlr.
25	Birnie, Patrick, horse-dealer		46	Kerr, A., temperance hotel
25	Ritchie, George		44	Wardale, T., & Son, sawmkrs.
27	Steedman, Adam		42	Hume, Elliot, drysalter
31	Main, A. & J., & Co., Corn Exchange Buildings		42	McCrae, George, hatter

Grassmarket, Edinburgh 1883-4

1	Richardson, Francis, & Co	60	M'Donald, Angus, saddler
5	Scott, James, & Co	56 & 58	Rose, William, saddler
7	Lindsay, John	54	Wilkinson, John
9	Spence, Joseph, saddler	54	Thomson's Court

We can see that in 1882-3, three saddlers, Joseph Spence, Angus M'Donald and William Rose, lived in the street. There is also a horse dealer, so we can see clearly the importance of horses to the town's trade.

If we compare this directory with the following year's, 1883-4, we learn that William Rose's business has been successful – he has bought number 56 from the rope, bag and twine store. You can see how documents like these really bring history to life.

A. & J. MAIN & CO.,

IRON FENCE, GATE, AND BRIDGE MANUFACTURERS,

WIRE-WORKERS, ETC.,

CORN EXCHANGE BUILDINGS, 31 GRASSMARKET

A. & J. MAIN & CO. supply every description of Garden Requisites, including—

Wire Archways and Flower Trainers,
Ornamental Iron and Wire Hurdles,
Flower Baskets and Stands in great variety,
Pea and Seed Protectors,
Garden Stakes and Pea Trainers
Floral Tools and Garden Hand Lights,
Garden Seats, Chairs, and Tables,
Lawn Mowers, Rollers, and Hose Reels,
Wrought-Iron Wine Bins,
Croquet and Lawn Tennis,
Improved Portable Steps for Libraries, etc.

All sorts of iron products were sold at number 31, Grassmarket. Are you surprised to see that lawnmowers and washing machines were on sale in 1883?

Galvanized Wire Netting, etc., fixed on Railings.

A. & J. M. & Co. also supply MANGLES, WRINGING and WASHING MACHINES, by all the Best Makers. Entrance and Field Gates, Iron and Steel Wire for Fencing Purposes, Game-Proof Wire Netting, etc. etc.

Price Lists supplied Free on application.

Look at the trades listed in these Edinburgh directory snippets from 1881 to 1884 for a street in Granton, which is north of Edinburgh on the Firth of Forth. Do you notice that a number of them are linked to the sea? Donald Macdonald was a boatman, W. Scott was a ship carpenter and William Morrison was a captain. People like the shore dues collector John Geddes worked as Customs officials, collecting tax on imported goods (H.M.C stands for Her Majesty's Customs). Clues from other sources would tell us that Granton in the 1880s was a small port, with a fleet of fishing boats.

Granton 1881-1882
(Cramond District)
Forth Place

Duncan, John, Maclean Cottage
5 Hartvig, Michael
3 Henderson, David
2 Blair, John
   Malcolm D. B., Wardie Hotel

East Cottages
M'Adie, Robert (H.M.C)
Geddes, John, shore dues collector
Macdonald, Donald, boatman
M'Kelvie, Archibald
M'Kelvie, Mrs, refreshment rooms
M'Adie, George (H.M.C)
Scott, W., ship carpenter
Landles, W., timber measurer
Morrison, Captain William

Granton 1882-1883
(Cramond District)
Forth Place

Duncan, John, Maclean Cottage
3 Henderson, David
2 Blair, John
   Malcolm D. B., Wardie Hotel

East Cottages
M'Adie, Robert (H.M.C)
Geddes, John, shore dues collector
Macdonald, Donald, boatman
M'Kelvie, Archibald
Scott, Miss C.
M'Adie, George (H.M.C)
Scott, W., ship carpenter
Landles, W., timber measurer
Reid, A., contractor
Morrison, Captain William

Granton 1883-1884
(Cramond District)
Forth Place

Duncan, John, Maclean Cottage
1 Paulin, John, coal mer.
2 Blair, John
4 Clephane, E.
5 Allan, David
   Malcolm D. B., Wardie Hotel, *Forth Corinthian Yacht Club.*

East Cottages
M'Adie, Robert (H.M.C)
Macdonald, Donald, boatman
M'Kelvie, Archibald
Scott, Miss C.
M'Adie, George (H.M.C)
Scott, W., ship carpenter
Landles, George (H.M.C.)
Landles, W., timber measurer
Reid, A., contractor
Morrison, Captain William

Advertisements like this, from the 1882 Edinburgh street directory, can add colour to your project.

This picture of Granton harbour in 1880 confirms the street directory evidence that the town was a fishing port.

You should ask yourself the following sorts of questions when using street directories:
- What was the most common occupation in the street?
- Which people advertised their businesses?
- Which people arrived in, or departed from, the street in a certain year?
- How long did a particular person live in their house?

To solve some mysteries, you need to look at street directories over a period of years. If you look at the Granton examples again, you will see that there were a number of changes in a three-year period. Archibald M'Kelvie's neighbour changes from Mrs M'Kelvie and her refreshment rooms to Miss C. Scott. Perhaps by looking at other clues, like censuses, we could solve the mystery of whether Archibald lost his mother or replaced his wife!

Look at the Granton street directory entries:
- ❖ What can you find out about W. Landles and John Geddes?
- ❖ What happened at D. B. Malcolm's hotel?

By looking at a series of street directories, a careful detective may be able to plot how many new houses were built in a street each year. As you can see from our example, the street directories can raise as many questions as they answer!

THE CENSUS

A census is a questionnaire that the government sends out to all householders every ten years. It started in 1801 and has continued up to 1991. The next one will be in 2001. All householders have to give information about themselves and all the people who live in their house. The census is therefore a very important source of clues about local history.

As history detectives, we can only investigate census material that is at least a hundred years old, because recent information is considered private. So, the latest census that we can read is 1891. Any census from around 1841 to 1891 is usually found in the main reference library in your area. A census from before 1841 was very basic and does not provide a great deal of information.

If we look at the census of Beenham, in Berkshire, for 1881, we can see how much information is available about a family in the past:

Road, Street or Name of House	Name and Surname	Relation to Head of family	Condition as to marriage	Age last birthday	Profession or occupation	Where born
Vicarage	Thomas H Bushnell	Head	Married	66	Vicar of Beenham	Berkshire Beenham
	Emily Bushnell	Wife	Married	76		
	Emily Bushnell	Daughter	Single	35		Berkshire, Beenham
	Margaret Bushnell	Daughter	Single	34		Berkshire, Beenham
	Lydia Smith	Servant	Single	30	Cook and domestic servant	Cambridgeshire Wisbeach
	Lucy Bosley	Servant	Single	40	Housemaid and domestic servant	Berkshire
	Louisa Ashby	Servant	Single	15	Domestic servant	Surrey

We know the names, ages, jobs and places of birth of everybody living in the house, in this case the vicarage. From the information we can work out the family relationships. This one is very simple.

We can find out the history of Beenham vicarage, shown above, by finding evidence in the census.

Further clues about Beenham can be found in inscriptions written on gravestones in the nearby churchyard.

Thomas and Emily Bushnell had two unmarried daughters, Emily and Margaret. Some census entries can be much more difficult than this, with sons and wives, daughters and husbands, and grandchildren all living in the same house. It is possible to draw simple family trees from the census information to work out the relationships.

✤ Look carefully at the census. What is the difference between the Bushnells and most modern families?

The Census and Towns

By investigating a complete census for a village or part of a town, it is possible to work out details about that town's history. For example, in a village you could find out how many people worked as farm labourers, and how many as domestic servants. You might find clues which suggest that the main craft of the village was rope-making, pottery or weaving.

1851 Abbeydale Census

Ecclesiastical District of Ecclesal   *Borough of Sheffield*

Name or No. of House	Name and Surname of each Person who abode in the house on the Night of the 30th March 1851	Relation to Head of Family	Condition	Age	Rank, Profession, Or Occupation	Where Born
1 Abbeydale Works	William Tyzack	Head	Married	35	Scythe Manufacturer Employing 30 Men	Yorks, Ecclesall
	Fanny Tyzack	Wife	Married	36		Derbyshire Norton
	Anne Tyzack	Daughter	Single	8		Yorks, Ecclesall
	Fanny Tyzack	Daughter	Single	6		"
	William Tyzack	Son	Single	4		"
	Frank Tyzack	Son	Single	6 mths		"
	Joshua Tyzack	Brother	Single	34		"
5 Abbeydale House	Robert Newbold	Head	Married	30	American Merchant in Cutlery	Warwicks, Coventry
	Avenilda Newbold	Wife	Married	26		Yorks, Sheffield
	Sarah Watkinson	Servant	Single	28	Servant, Cook	Yorks, Sheffield
	Elisa Bolsover	Servant	Single	24	Housemaid	Derbys, Norton
	James Cope	Servant	Single	28	Groom	Shrops, Shrews.
7 Abbeydale	Thomas Greaves	Head	Married	26	Scythe Smith	Derbys, Norton
	Hannah Greaves	Wife	Married	24		Yorks.
	Elisa Greaves	Daughter	Single	3		Derbys, Norton
	Thomas Greaves	Son	Single	3 mths		Yorks, Ecclesall

The original censuses were all hand-written and are sometimes difficult to read. You have to study them closely to find the clues that you need. The information above was taken from the census for Abbeydale in 1851.

If you look at the Abbeydale census, you will see that 35-year-old Mr Tyzack is a scythe manufacturer, and Thomas Greaves, who lives at number 7, Abbeydale, is a scythe smith.

- Why is the job of Robert Newbold, from Abbeydale House, interesting in a study of Abbeydale's history?
- Find Norton, Ecclesall, Abbeydale and Sheffield on a map. Were most people born close to Abbeydale?
- When do you think the Greaves family moved to the district of Ecclesall?

Further study of the census will show that the industrial centre of Abbeydale was a steel mill, where steel was forged into scythes. This information can be supported by finding the remains of the mill or old photographs of the furnace. You can see how a history detective rebuilds the past by using census information.

If you decide to use census material for your project and you have access to a computer at home or at school, you could put the information on to a simple database for future reference.

The blacksmith shown above was painted in 1771 by Joseph Wright in Derby, not far from Abbeydale.

Compare the blacksmith with this modern photograph of the working remains of the forge at Abbeydale. You can see how the steel mill must have changed the lives of the people in the census.

SCHOOL LOGBOOKS

These girls of class II were photographed at Ackworth Girls' School in 1899. You may be able to find a logbook from the same year that mentions some of them.

Did you know that since Victorian times, head teachers have written down in diaries all the events, special holidays, illnesses, punishments and other information that has affected their school? These diaries are called school logbooks, and are excellent sources for your local history project.

Logbooks can inform the history detective about the day-to-day running of a school, the type of lessons taught and the number of pupils attending the school. They can also show a pattern of events over a long period of time. This pattern can reveal the different problems, such as poor roads and bad weather, that affected school attendance in the area.

The examples on the opposite page are taken from logbooks in different primary schools in Kent, Hampshire and Berkshire. They will give you an idea of the sorts of details that such documents can provide. Note that some of this information can lead you on to further study. Some of the names mentioned can be checked on the census, allowing you to find out about a child's family.

2 October 1882
Typhoid fever has broken out in the area.

15 March 1895
For the past week or more I have distributed daily doses of ammoniated tincture of quinine to many children affected with colds and in many cases with beneficial results.

9 October 1882
It was found that 130 children were suffering from Measles. The school was closed.

17 June 1887
Many fainting fits over the past few weeks, the most serious of which, Claire Luckin, apparently fresh and healthy at school on May 16 and taken ill during the night, died on May 31 of 'inflammation of the brain'.

It is interesting to see how common some illnesses were in past years and the number of times schools had to be closed because of them. They included everything from the common cold to typhoid, diptheria, 'brain fever', scarlet fever and ringworm.

– How do you think illnesses in Victorian times compare with those that schoolchildren suffer from today?
– What other examples can you find in a local logbook?

If you could find out the names of children in a Victorian school photograph like this one, and look them up in a logbook, you could create a fascinating project.

Attendances

Logbooks show that illness was not the only thing that kept children away from school. They also give you clues about the bribes and rewards which were given to those who made an effort to attend:

27 February 1874	*Owing to the rain the night of the 26th many of the roads were flooded and many children were not able to attend school.*
18 December 1876	*Annie Frost still away ... to look after younger sister who is also staying away because she has no shoes.*
2 January 1877	*It was decided at the last committee meeting to present with a half-penny each child who attends school and is present at prayers every time the school is opened during the week.*
19 November 1898	*Today tea was given to 153 children who never missed an attendance in the year ending 31 October 1898. Medals for regular attendance were presented by Mrs Nicholson. Alfred Cooyer received his seventh medal.*

17 April 1872
Thin attendance this week on account of hop-tying.

6 October 1873
Attendance low due to hop-picking.

25 April 1875
Many boys absent helping erect the hop-poles.

24 August 1945
School closed today because of the hop-picking.

Some events affecting attendance occur regularly over a number of years. In Victorian times, it was common for children to go to work as well as attend school. In Kent, picking hops was a popular way to earn extra money.

These schoolchildren in 1901 did not even change out of uniform before picking hops to earn extra money.

3 August 1874	*Attendance low. The reason: a Grand Circus being at Tunbridge Wells and a cricket match at Penshurst.*
3 November 1873	*Visitors. His Grace the Archbishop of Canterbury visited the school today.*
1946	*Funeral of Field Marshall Lord Gort VC. Children watched the cortege as the military funeral is of historical interest.*

Special Events

Extracts from logbooks can also reveal the social events and customs which were important to the local area in the past. Travelling circuses were very popular and you may come across references to them in the logbooks. Remember, there was no television, so a visiting circus was a very important source of entertainment for many people.

Any of these logbook entries could be a starting point for your project, especially if you want to study the social life in your town during the last century.

Where do you find the logbook? Recent logbooks will be kept at their school. Older ones will be at the local Record Office, and can be found using the process described in Chapter Three.

In Victorian times, the circus coming to town was a good enough excuse to stay away from school.

PHOTOGRAPHS

Throughout this book, we have used photographs to illustrate the chapters. But how useful are they and how can a history detective use them?

Look at these two photographs of St Leonard's Square, in Wallingford, Oxfordshire. The bottom picture was taken around 1910 and shows the Methodist Chapel and the Free Library and Literary Institute. The top photograph was taken in 1996. You would have expected a lot of changes to have taken place in eighty years, but if you look carefully the site is almost exactly the same.

❀ What clues tell you that the colour photograph shows the square in 1996?

St Leonard's Square, Wallingford, photographed in 1996 (left).

St Leonard's Square, as it looked in 1910 (below).

When you look at a photograph you need to ask yourself two basic questions:

– What does the photographer want me to see in this photograph? This is called the witting testimony. It is the main subject of the photo. It could be a person, a building, an event or anything which the photographer actually wanted to capture on film.

– What else is there in the picture that is useful to me as a historian? This is called the unwitting testimony. It is any detail which the photographer included by accident.

Wallingford Market Square, photographed in 1996

Both witting and unwitting testimony can be very useful if you are investigating how an area has changed over a number of years.

The two photographs on this page show Wallingford Market Square. You can see a little more change in these pictures, especially in the street on the left. Notice the new style of buildings in the modern picture.

What clues help you to date the older picture? Look at the car in the background and the clothes the people are wearing. If you visited the site, you would find out that the fountain in the middle of the square was built in 1885.

Wallingford Market Square, as it looked in 1910.

PHOTOGRAPHS

A simple 'snap' taken on holiday of a family on the beach may not seem at first sight to be very useful. However, if you look beyond the main subject you may see:
– what the weather was like
– what people were wearing and eating
– makes of cars and buses

You may be able to use your detective skills to date a photograph from objects you see in the background. For instance, if you know that a particular car was produced in 1950 and you can see it in the picture, you can be sure that the photo was taken during or after 1950.

Old postcards can be very useful to your study. They can be found at markets, antique fairs and car-boot sales. We can use them to see what life was like at a particular time in history. Sometimes the dates are written on them. If not, there are usually enough clues to help us identify when the photo for the postcard was taken.

A postcard of London.

THE PROMENADE & NORTH HILL, MINEHEAD.

206,893 ④

A postcard of Minehead.

Look at the postcard showing London. We know from the clock and the daylight that it is 11.15 am. Look at the transport – there is not a car in sight. It is helpful when examining smaller pictures to use a magnifying glass. This would help you see what the carts are carrying. Can you see the open-topped bus and the hansom cab? By looking up illustrations of the clothes in reference books we could work out that this picture was taken in the late nineteenth or early twentieth century. This is where your detective skills become useful!

Look at the postcard showing Minehead, and see from the clues available if you can work out the following:

🐾 What was the weather like?
🐾 What type of people went to Minehead for their holidays?
🐾 What is attached to the tree on the left?
🐾 What do you think the lady right of centre is pushing?
🐾 How can we date the photograph?

VILLAGE PATTERNS

Even if you decide to study a single building or a particular street, you will find it helpful to investigate how the surrounding community came to exist in the first place. To find out about the community's earliest history, you should ask yourself:
– Why was a village founded on this site?
– How did the village or town change and develop?

Towns and villages were established for many different reasons, but if a settlement was to survive for a long time it needed to supply the basic needs of its inhabitants. If you had been one of the first people to settle in your area you would have needed:
– material to build your house
– somewhere to get your water
– pasture for your animals
– a source of heat
You may also have needed to live somewhere which could be easily defended against other groups of people.

Many towns in Wales developed because coal was discovered. Mining became the traditional skill of inhabitants like these workmen from Bwllfa Colliery, in Aberdare.

A site providing all these basic requirements would be located near:
– a river for water
– a wood for building materials and fuel
– a hill or a junction in a river, which could be easily defended

Some early sites did not survive. There could have been many different reasons for this. Perhaps all the trees were chopped down or the water became infected. The inhabitants could have become ill and the community simply died out – perhaps during a plague like the Black Death in 1348.

Smoke pours from the chimneys in 1920, when Glamorgan was a growing town, because of its rich seams of coal.

Other communities may have flourished. The soil might have been particularly suitable for growing crops, and encouraged farmers to settle there. Perhaps coal, iron ore, tin or other minerals were found in the ground, and a community grew up around the mine.

This is Glamorgan in 1967, after the mines had been shut down. The large building on the left appears on the right of the photograph above. The machinery and railway at the front of the old photograph have vanished.

The photographs of Welsh mining towns in this chapter show how a community might grow and then decline. When a mine was first established, the owners needed some way of getting the coal from the site. Originally they used horses and carts. After the 1840s a railway might have been built to make the journey easier.

A pit pony hauling coal at Pontypool in 1910.

Simple cottages were built near mines and rented out by the mine owners to their workers. The miners also needed churches to go to each Sunday, a school for their children and shops to buy their groceries. There would also have been houses for the mine owner, doctor, schoolmaster and vicar to live in.

A foundation stone shows this mine was opened in 1925. It had closed down before this 1967 photograph was taken.

Today, because of the expense of getting the coal above ground, a lot of mines lie closed. The original village might now be part of a larger town. The original railway line may have been taken up during the 'Beeching Cuts' of the 1960s, when many stations were closed down by Lord Beeching.

You can find clues by looking at foundation stones of buildings with either the name of the original mine or the initials NCB. This stands for the National Coal Board, which took over independent mines in 1947. A stone with the original mine's name without the initials NCB, had to be there before 1947.

Some old stations, churches, chapels and schools are now private houses. If you have any in your local area, they would make an excellent starting point for a study. Careful investigation of maps, old photographs and documents will help you to piece together a town's history of growth and decline.

Duffryn Rhondda Colliery, abandoned in 1972. The railway which once linked Swansea and the Rhondda Valley lies closed. Only the steps help to show that the two photographs on this page were taken at the same place.

The same colliery, when it was a working industry in 1924.

BUILDINGS

Vital clues to the history and growth of a settlement can be found in objects that you see every day and probably take for granted – buildings.

– Have you ever looked carefully at the buildings in your area?
– What clues do you think can help you to work out their age?

Most buildings in your town are probably built from brick or stone. Before the 1600s, however, most houses were built from wood, which was easily available. Because wood rots, not many of these houses have survived in their original form.

Stone and bricks were expensive before the seventeenth century. They were usually used only for important buildings such as the church or the lord of the manor's house. Some of these buildings have survived until today, as the oldest buildings in their area.

By the late seventeenth century, more buildings were being built from stone. The type of stone used depended on what was available in the local area.

Little Moreton Hall, in Congleton, Cheshire, was built in the fifteenth century when wood was the cheapest building material.

Before canals and roads were built it was very difficult to move stone over muddy tracks. In some areas, complete streets of houses, often all owned by one landlord, were built from the same local material and to the same design. You can see examples of these in Royal Crescent, Bath.

There was another big change in building styles during the Industrial Revolution of the eighteenth and nineteenth centuries. The use of iron became fashionable. Iron bridges, railings and decorations changed the appearance of the country. People from villages moved to cities to find work in the iron and coal-mining industries. They needed homes close to their work, so rows and rows of terraced houses were built. After 1830, the new railways allowed people to travel to work from further away. People now began to live on the outskirts of cities, in areas that became known as suburbs.

These eighteenth-century houses in Bath were built out of stone from local quarries.

Architecture is quite a complicated subject, but these pictures should help you find clues to identifying the age of local buildings.

Before 1465

Small houses are made from wood, with no foundations and roofs covered in thatch or split stone. In areas where it was easy to get, houses were built from local stone – particularly by the Normans.

Tudor 1485-1603

Wooden Tudor buildings tend to sag in the middle, because of poor foundations. The top floors often hang over the ones below. Doors are small. On average the people in the Tudor period were shorter than today's population. Windows are of uneven shapes, with small panes because glass was so expensive.

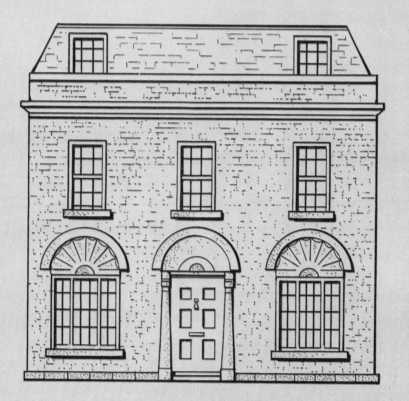

Georgian 1714-1830

In 1666, the Great Fire of London destroyed many wooden houses. The terraced, stone houses with classical designs which replaced them, created the Georgian style. These bigger, symmetrical houses have large windows with small, rectangular panes, opened by ropes called 'sash cords'. There are often windows called 'fan-lights' over the front door.

Victorian 1837-1901
Mostly built from brick, many Victorian houses have slate roofs. Workers' terraced houses, often 'two-up, two-down' homes (two rooms on each floor), are built in cities. Some later buildings have bay windows and decorated brickwork. Public buildings have decorated roofs. Many schools were built around 1870, and many churches were rebuilt or altered in Victorian times.

1900-1940
Houses are built of brick, sometimes decorated with 'pebble-dash'. Many windows open sideways. Roofs are often tiled. Front doors have coloured glass in the upper half, and porches are fashionable. From 1936, many houses are built with garages. The first council-house estates are built on the edges of towns and cities.

1940-Today
Red-brick houses are built with large 'picture windows', often with garages. Use of steel and concrete allows the construction of taller buildings like high-rise flats. More modern houses have no chimney, because they use oil, gas or electric heating. Many small shops are closed and converted into houses.

A Secret Code

If you choose to study the buildings in your area, it is useful to write the details of each building on a map. There is not space to write down the details in full, so instead the history detective can write them in a secret code. Using this code, you can use a single symbol to show these six features of a building:

– **MATERIAL:** What is it made from?
– **ROOF:** What is the roof covered with?
– **STOREYS:** How many floors does it have?
– **TYPE:** Is it detached, semi-detached or terraced?
– **USE:** What is it used for?
– **AGE:** How old is it?

Firstly, we have to give each feature a key, so that we know what the codes mean:

🐾 Who lives in this building? There is a big clue in the picture.

Material
1. Brick
2. Stone
3. Wood
4. Flint
5. Brick & Stone
6. Brick & Wood
7. Other

Roof
A. Tile
B. Slate
C. Split stone
D. Thatch

Storeys
1. One storey
2. Two storeys
3. Three storeys

Type
A. Detached
B. Semi-detached
C. Terraced

Use
1. House
2. Church
3. Pub
4. Community Hall
5. School
6. Shop
7. Other

Age
A. Before 1500
B. Tudor
C. Georgian
D. Victorian
E. Edwardian
F. Modern

Now we have our codes, how are they used? We simply look at a building and write down the codes of its features *in the correct order*. The codes for the building in this photograph would create a symbol that looks like this:

5 D 2
A I B

The first three codes are written on the top, the second three on the bottom. The code holds all this information about the building:

MATERIAL	ROOF	STOREYS
Brick and stone	Thatch	Two
5	**D**	**2**
A	**I**	**B**
Detached	House	Tudor
TYPE	USE	AGE

When you look at a building you can quickly write down its secret code. When you get back home, the codes of different buildings can be marked on a map like the one below. You can then compare your map with old maps of the area, which you can find in your local library. Maps from certain years may confirm your own findings about the historical buildings in your area.

You may want to make up your own secret code, describing other features such as windows, chimneys or gardens.

– Write down a description of the buildings marked by the codes on this map:

This thatched cottage has its own secret code.

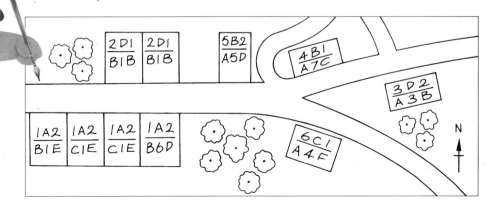

INTERVIEWING WITNESSES

Have you ever spoken to your grandparents about what life was like in the past? You can find out a great deal about your local area by talking to people who have lived there for a long time. They may have owned the local shop or gone to the local school. Your grandparents may be able to describe what life was like in their home town during World War II.

Before you interview somebody, make sure that you are fully prepared. Try to think of some interesting questions that might uncover important clues about your history project. If you have a tape recorder, you could ask your subject's permission to record your interview. Otherwise, you should take some notes from their answers.

Your granny may have some interesting memories of life during World War II.

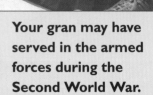

Your gran may have served in the armed forces during the Second World War.

The questions you ask should be connected to the project you are doing. You may find that once your subject starts talking, they talk about all sorts of different things. Do not worry about this, as they may provide you with some material that you had not even thought about.

You need to check any information carefully, and try to support it with evidence from other sources. Memories can sometimes be unreliable, and people tend to recall only the good or bad things that have happened to them. If they are remembering things from a long time ago, they may also be unclear about dates.

You may find that someone's memories of the past can provide you with a much stronger sense of history than you could ever get by reading a book. You might also discover things about your local history that no other detective knows.

Some people's grans will remember helping the war effort by joining the **Women's Land Army**.

☙ **Why do you think this cow was painted white during the German bombing campaign, known as the Blitz?**

THE CHURCH

There are a lot of clues to be found in a church, particularly if it is an old building. Churches are full of memorials. If you read some of them carefully, you may be able to draw simple family trees from the names mentioned on them. They might also tell you the jobs of people in the area, which you could compare with jobs mentioned in the local censuses.

On the outside of United Reformed, Baptist and Methodist churches, you can often see foundation stones which will give you a very important clue to when the chapel was built. It will also tell you who it was that laid the original stone.

If you ask, you may be able to see some of the church records. These often include a list of all the clergymen in the church's history.

To follow a trail deeper into the past we can study writing on monuments like the one above, which is in Edinburgh. Using a magnifying glass, find out how and when the Marquis of Argyle died.

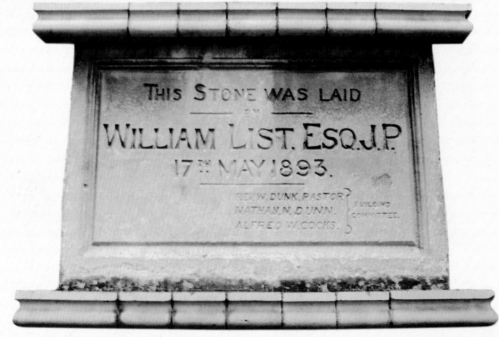

❀ What was the job of William List, who laid this church foundation stone?

Such documents can give you a good idea of how long the church has been there. This is also a clue to how long there has been a community in the area. The church was a very important building in the early history of a settlement. Remember that the church building you see today may not be the one that was originally built on the site.

Often you will find written histories on sale in the church. Guidebooks may provide information about the buildings, memorials and stained-glass windows.

❧ This is a 'sanctuary knocker' from a church door in Whalley, Lancashire. What do you think it was used for?

Records in Eyam Church, Derbyshire (right), show that plague killed 262 of Eyam's 350 inhabitants in 1665.

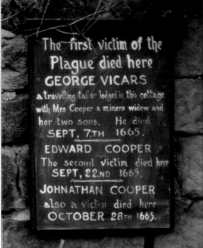

The first victim of the Plague died here
GEORGE VICARS
a travelling tailor lodged in this cottage with Mrs Cooper a miners widow and her two sons. He died
SEPT. 7.TH 1665.
EDWARD COOPER
The second victim died here
SEPT. 22.ND 1665.
JOHNATHAN COOPER
also a victim died here
OCTOBER 28TH 1665.

❧ Church records can be supported by other clues. What was the job of the first plague victim in Eyam?

OTHER CLUES

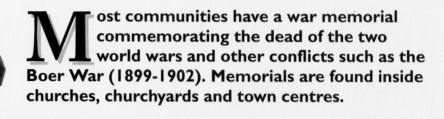

Most communities have a war memorial commemorating the dead of the two world wars and other conflicts such as the Boer War (1899-1902). Memorials are found inside churches, churchyards and town centres.

The names of people killed in the Boer War and the First World War (1914-18) can be traced back to the census material of 1871-1891. This makes it possible to work out their family background. Studying the soldiers' backgrounds in censuses and street directories makes you realize that they are more than just names inscribed on the memorial.

Community and village halls can also provide clues to local history. They were often built for a purpose. A clue to this may be found in their name, or the date when they were built. For example, a building called Jubilee Hall built in 1897 was erected to celebrate the diamond jubilee of Queen Victoria. A modern building called Jubilee Hall was probably built in 1977 to celebrate the silver jubilee of Queen Elizabeth II.

Some of the names on this memorial (left) to the soldiers who died in the First World War may also be found in the censuses and street directories of 1871-1891. By finding them, you could show how the war affected the local families and community.

What does this flying fish from Edinburgh advertise?

What could you buy from the shop under this sign?

Where would you find a shop sign like this one?

There are clues to our local history all around us. Other useful sources include inns and public houses, memorial gardens, inscriptions, shop signs, statues and clocks. Useful secondary sources include parish magazines, church magazines, church histories and books written about an area by its inhabitants.

SOLVING THE MYSTERY

You should now be able to find the clues to solve your own history mystery. To help you enjoy making your own local history project, here is a list of things to remember:

- Study something that is within easy reach of your home.
- Try to plan your topic before you start hunting for clues.
- Check the best time to visit churches, libraries and Record Offices. Some places are closed at weekends, so it may be best to do your project during school holidays when you can visit places during the week.
- When you find a document or photograph, make a note of where you found it and what date it was written or taken.
- Remember to think about how an area has changed during its history. Include as many aspects of life as possible.

In your completed project, you could include investigations of:
- the history of buildings and the development of a settlement
- the changing inhabitants of a street
- a particular building such as a church, manor or mill
- the history of a school and its pupils
- the influence of a particular family in the area
- an industry, trade or craft

This is an old photograph of an oast house in Paddock Wood, Kent. Many oasts have now been converted into houses, like that shown on page 4.

These men are loading hops into an oast house, to be dried and brewed into beer. Compare the towers to those on page 4.

When a detective has gathered all his clues together, it is important that he or she presents the evidence clearly. When you write up your project, use neatly drawn maps with a title, key and scale. Use photographs and pictures, and give them each a title and a date. If you choose a topic that you find interesting, then other people will enjoy reading it. Above all, ENJOY YOURSELF!

Good hunting!

GLOSSARY

archivist Someone responsible for looking after the documents in a Record Office.

Blitz German air raids on London in World War II.

brain fever Inflammation of the brain.

colliery A coal mine.

Customs Government department which stops goods being smuggled into the country.

detached (A house) Standing on its own.

diptheria An infectious disease of the throat.

family trees Charts showing family relationships.

foundations The base of a building.

hansom cab A two-wheeled, horse-drawn cab.

Industrial Revolution The rapid development of British industry in the 1700s and 1800s.

inflammation Redness, swelling and pain, caused by infection.

jubilee An anniversary celebration, for example a diamond jubilee (sixty or seventy years) or a silver jubilee (twenty-five years).

manor A large country estate.

marquis A nobleman.

oast house A building used for drying hops.

parish The smallest area with a local or church council.

pithead The top of a mine shaft, and the buildings surrounding it.

primary source Historical information that comes from the actual time.

quinine A bitter substance used as a medicine.

Record Office A government office where important local records are stored.

ringworm A very contagious disease that affects the skin, causing circular, bare patches.

scarlet fever A disease marked by fever and a red rash.

scythe An agricultural tool with a long, curved handle.

secondary source Historical information written after the period it describes.

semi-detached (A house) Joined on one side.

terraced (A house) Joined on both sides.

typhoid A very infectious disease causing severe diarrhoea and weakness.

BOOKS TO READ

It is difficult to give you a general reading list, because the books you need will depend on the project you decide to do. Instead, here are a few hints to help you find the information that you require.

You may find that a local historian or history group has already done some work in your area, and you can use their research as a secondary source for your project. Most libraries have a section on local history. Once you have started your project, you will find that you need other books to provide you with extra details. Again, get these from a library because many are expensive, and you may need to read only a few pages. Take a note of the title, author and library reference number, in case you need to get the book again.

There are a number of books that deal with specific subjects, such as churches and memorials. It is also worth having your own pocket guide to architecture to help you find out the date of buildings. You should be able to find one in your local bookshop.

If you decide to study your local area at a certain time in history then books providing a general background to the period would be useful. For example, the Wayland 'Victorian Life' series will help you to investigate your own area in the nineteenth century, and compare the information with its historical background.

Page 5:

❧ The pub sign shows beer barrels and sheaves of barley, which are used to brew beer.

❧ Brewing was an important Kentish industry. The oast houses were used to dry the hops which flavoured the beer. These were picked from the hop fields shown on the signpost, and made into beer by the 'brewers' shown on the pub sign.

Page 7:

❧ Woodley Aerodrome existed near Reading. The streets are all named after types of aeroplane. The pub sign shows a Spitfire, and the newspaper headline is about the Royal Air Force in World War II.

Page 8:

❧ The well was a gift from a 'maharajah' or prince in India, who had heard from a visiting Oxfordshire man that Stoke Row was suffering from a water shortage!

Page 9:

❧ The signs were fire marks to show which insurance company a house was insured with. In the seventeenth century, each insurance company had its own fire brigade, who would put out your fire only if your house was displaying their fire mark!

Page 11:

❧ The reference number for Crookham School in Thatcham is C/EL36/1-3.

Page 15:

❧ W. Landles was resident in Granton from 1881-4. In 1883-4, a relative, George Landles, seems to have moved in with him. John Geddes no longer lived in Granton after 1883.

❧ The hotel started the Forth Corinthian Yacht Club in 1883-4.

Page 17:

❧ The Bushnell family had servants.

Page 19:

❧ Robert Newbold's job as American Merchant in Cutlery shows us how important foreign trade was to Abbeydale.

❧ Yes, people did not generally move so far from home in 1851.

❧ (page 19) The Greaves family probably moved within the last three years, as their three-year-old daughter was born in Norton, the hometown of Thomas Greaves.

Page 24:

❧ The ivy-covered building now houses an electronics firm. The car, road signs, clothes, street lights and television aerials are all modern.

Page 27:

❧ The shadows show the weather was sunny.

❧ Most of the people are well-dressed, probably from the middle classes.

❧ A magnifying glass will show you a weighing machine beside the tree.

❧ She is pushing a pram.

❧ The style of clothes - the ladies' dresses and hats, the men's hats and shoes - are the best clues, suggesting the 1920s or 1930s.

Page 36:

❧ Doves live in this building, called a dove-cote.

Page 39:

❧ To stop German bombers seeing their targets, people were forbidden to use lights. This was called the 'blackout'. Even motorists had to drive without lights, so the farmer thought his cow was less likely to be run over if it was painted white!

Page 40:

❧ He was a J.P., or Justice of the Peace, which means a magistrate.

Page 41:

❧ Criminals in medieval times were granted the Church's protection from the law if they struck the knocker.

❧ George Vicars was a travelling tailor.

Page 43:

❧ The top-left sign is a mortar and pestle from a chemist's shop.

❧ The three brass balls are the traditional sign for a pawnbroker's, which lends money to people but takes their property until the loan is repaid with interest.

❧ The flying fish advertises a fishmonger's.

INDEX